100

D0352424

ISBN 1 871964 00 8

Illustrations by Ian O'Sullivan
Cover designed by C.P.S., Portsmouth.
Printed in Hong Kong.

dedicated
to all the girls I wish I'd known

preface

Throughout history men and women have gone to great lengths to make complete asses of themselves in order to meet. I guess with a book like this, things will now be somewhat different. Men and women can now look forward to making complete asses of themselves in style.

To write a book like this, one must either be the authority on the subject, with great knowledge and experience on the psychological and psychoanalytic responses of human behaviour; or he or she must be completely and absolutely bonkers. As you go through this book you will discover that I am without a doubt the latter. In fact I would go as far as to say that I am probably the least qualified person to write a book on this subject, but at least I had the nerve to attempt it; which is precisely what is needed at the outset of any relationship. Body chemistry takes over the rest.

... And if this book helps to bring a smile to a few faces, or even succeeds to join two people together, then it hasn't been a complete waste of time.

acknowledgments

I would like to thank everyone who has helped to make this book possible.

I am grateful to the writers and poets, in particular those of the 16th and 17th century, whose work have inspired me, and some of which I have adapted to fit the realm of this book.

I like to thank Ian O'Sullivan for the great illustrations which give a totally new dimension to some of the lines.

But most of all, I must thank all those great looking guys who always managed to get the girls without having to utter a word. They gave us the not so good looking guys like myself the opportunity to stand in a corner desperately trying to think of chat up lines which could hopefully compensate for our looks.

Well here are the lines I thought of... They never did compensate for my looks. I hope they do for you.

contents

While reciting this poem, present her with flowers and presents. If she still refuses to have a drink with you, then seriously consider changing your soap brand.

❝ Flowers, presents, and a heart as true
The earth, the moon, and humour too
All these things I'll give to you
for a little chat and a drink or two. ❞

If the girl you wish to meet is looking somewhat glum, this line may help to break the ice... Or even your head depending on your luck.

I bet you have the kind of smile that lights up a room like a one million watts bulb.

Then as soon as she smiles, continue by saying:

mmmm... I guess I was wrong. But that's O.K. candle light is cool.

If you have the nerve, then try this one;

How about coming up to my place for a spot of heavy breathing?

Make sure she appreciates the fact that you live on the top floor flat of a block without lifts.

Go over to the one who has captured your heart, and say;

If you take my heart by surprise, don't you think the rest of my body has the right to follow?

Go over to her staring into her eyes, and say;

Well don't look so surprised. I would have thought with eyes like that, you would be used to guys coming up to you for a closer look. The question is, has anyone ever got close enough to drown in them. I know I want to.

Have this little message sent to the girl you haven't yet met, giving her yet another chance to discover that may be you are not such a bad guy to have around after all.

> **Boy sees girl. Girl sees boy.**
> **Boy likes girl. Girl is not so sure.**
> **Then girl phones boy. And now both**
> **are sure.**
>
> **Name** ....
>
> **Tel. No.** ....

Have a red rose and the following poem sent to
that special person you wish to meet.

❝ Bid me to live, and I will live
Your companion to be:
Or bid me love, and I will give
A loving heart to thee.

A heart as soft, a heart as kind,
A heart as sound and free
As in the whole world you cannot
find,
that heart I'll give to thee.

Bid that heart stay, and it will stay,
to honour thy decree:
or bid it languish quite away,
and it shall do so for thee.

Bid me to weep, and I will weep
While I have eyes to see:
And having none, yet I will keep
A heart to weep for thee.

Continued...

" Bid me despair, and I'll despair,
under that cypress tree:
or bid me die, and I will dare
the end death, to die for thee.

You are my life, my love, my
heart,
The very eyes of me,
And have command of every part,
To live and die for thee.

Yet to this day we haven't met
Which I find sad to see:
To have this love, and be set,
But not be given to thee.

So please please please remember
you can set this love free
...... is my name,
and ...... is my number,
The next move is left to thee. "

Adapted from a peom by Robert Herrick 1634

This one may make her feel so guilty that she will surrender and have a drink with you, just to cheer you up.

Go near the person you wish to have a drink with, Stand where she might accidentally knock into you. As soon as she does, bend down as if you were looking for something, at the same time asking her if she would help you look for your contact lenses.

If all else fails to get a dance, lie, lie, lie.

66 I am a private investigator on a top secret mission. I think I am being watched, so please will you dance with me, because if I dance on my own, it might look suspicious, and it may blow my cover.

MI5 would be grateful for your cooperation. 99

If smiles have been exchanged, but the circumstances do not allow for anything further, then write this message on a piece of paper and hand it over to her;

**66 How delicious is the winning
of a kiss at love's beginning
when two mutual hearts are sighing
for the knot there is no untying.
So dial my number and keep it
ringing,
and I'll tell you why I've been
grinning.**

Name .... **Tel. No.** **99**

Try adding a few more lines to this one and go for the kill by boredom. She will give up on life and accept anything that comes her way...even you.

> Please forgive me for intruding on you like this; but if I don't stop you now, I may never run into you again, and I may never have the pleasure of knowing who you are, so that we can fulfil our destiny together on this planet.

Go over to the girl you wish to meet, and try your corniest line;

> If I said you had a cute little body, would you hold it against me?

Go up to the one you wish to disgust and say;

> **Gifted as I am, with beauty that probably no other man on earth can rival... it is my hideous destiny to be madly loved at first sight by every woman I come across.**
> **........ well ??????**

Go up to him/her and say;

> **What is irritating above love is that it is a crime that requires an accomplice. So how would you like to be my partner in crime?**

*If you can't decide what line to use, then try this
one;*

I have been sitting over there, watching
you and wondering what kind of line I
could use which would be worthy of your
beauty without it being too soppy. When
all of a sudden it came to me, so here I
am to say it.
Ah... Ah... would you believe it? It's gone
again. Give me a few minutes I am sure
it will come back to me. Meanwhile can
I buy you a drink?

If you are not sure whether you are her kind of guy, then try this one;

Do you go for suave, sophisticated filthy rich intellectuals, with a great sense of humour and a bubbly personality?

If her answer is 'yes', continue by saying;

In that case would you like to drink?

If her answer is 'no', say;

Good, cause I ain't any of them. What are you drinking darling?

Go up to the girl you wish to meet, give her a rose, and say;

Hi... This bud is for you, and I must say that rose goes magnificently with your pale skin, dark eyes, white teeth and red lips. Can I ask you a question? What do you think of a perfect stranger coming up to you and giving you a rose? Ah... Yeh... But you mustn't underestimate the power of a stranger with a rose. I say that because I have a vested interest in meeting strangers. You see, every woman that I have ever liked, communed with or given off as a stranger, and only became known to me because I followed the impulse that I felt when I saw her, and I went up to her and I said 'Hi, my name is... I like you. Do you like me'.

*Go over to the girl you wish to meet, while holding
a copy of The Guiness Book of Records, and say;*

I don't know if you are familiar with the
rules and regulations about appearing in
the Guiness Book of Records. Apparently
if you think you are the tallest, shortest
or the fattest person in the world, you can
apply to break the record. But there is
one thing you cannot apply yourself to
challenge the record. And that is for
being the greatest lover in the world. For
that someone has to nominate you. So I
was wondering if you would nominate
me. Obviously I wouldn't want you to lie,
so I will give you all the time you need
to discover for yourself if I have a change
to break the record. In return I promise
not to leave you once I am rich and
famous.

Go up to the girl you wish to meet, and recite this poem. Make sure there are others around so that she gets embarrassed enough to surrender.

66 I am not a poet
As you will see
I musn't blow it
So please don't flee.

I wrote this poem
To ask you out
I'll even show 'em
So watch me shout:

I love this girl with all my heart
so give me a chance before we
part. **99**

This one is for the artists amongst you;

Wow that is a phenomenal smile. Has anyone ever told you that you look like a picasso painting?

She will probably reply **No**

Then continue by saying:

Why, are you an artist yourself?

She will again say **No**

Then pay her another compliment, and hope she will fall for this one:

I am, and I have never seen a subject as beautiful as you, and it's the ultimate desire of every artist to be given the opportunity to capture such beauty on canvas.

Then try and arrange a sitting and sketch away, but don't show her the work until she has fallen in love with you, and can accept you for the con artist that you are.

If circumstances forbid you to speak to the person with whom you have exchanged signs of mutual approval, then try sending her/him this message;

66 **Our eyes have met**
   Our hearts have spoken
   So please don't let
   The spell be broken

   Phone me later
   So we can meet
   To compare data
   On our heart beat. 99

Go up to the guy you wish to meet and say;

> **I am writing a book on some of the best chat up line you men have tried on us. Suppose you want to impress me, what would be your best chat up line?**

Then whatever he says, continue by saying;

> **O.K. I am impressed. Take me. I am yours.**

Go up to the guy you wish to meet, give him a bar of soap, and say;

O.K. so women can't help acting on impulse either.

Make sure you get the timing right for this one;

Please forgive me for intruding on you like this; but I have this problem. You see, one look at you and I have this funny feeling in my tummy. Now, I am either starving, or else I have fallen madly in love with you. And the only way I am going to find out is if you agree to have dinner with me.

If you like to invite her over to your table for a drink, try sending her this poem; but make sure her eyes are blue.

❝ Your eyes are blue
And I love you

Your smile is there
Is it for me?
My smile replies
To you from me.

Today and Always
I'll think of you
Your eyes I love
To look at you

I feel Giddy
To think that you
May come to me
For a drink or two. ❞

Go up to her, pretending to have difficulty standing up, and say;

This is the third time I have seen you, and the third time I have felt an almost paralising weakness in my knees; and I bet you haven't even noticed me once. That's why I have decided to come over and warn you that if you don't do anything about this, the next time I see you I may, just may go paralised and you would have to live the rest of your life with the guilt of putting someone in a wheelchair. So wouldn't it be better to let me buy you a drink now, while I can still walk.

Go up to her with a surprise look on your face and ask:

So where did you learn to do that?

To which she will probably reply,

What?

Then tell her,

**Hypnotising people with your eyes. I gaz-
ed in your eyes for a few moments, and
now feel completely hypnotised, and
ready to respond to your every command, whatever it may be."**

*Just hope that none of her commands include you
getting lost. Others you can probably handle.*

*If that special message is hard to put in your own
words, try this;*

   **❝ Come, thou Fairest Masterpiece
Of nature's work, her golden fleece:
Let me enjoy thee. flowers will fade
If not refreshed. Die not a maid;
Let us agree to appoint a day
To gather flowers. Why should
     you stay
So long a virgin? What have you
     done
To nature and yourself? A nun
Deserves not beauty. It is a mate
makes Cupid's darlings fortunate.
Since youth and beauty then invite
you thus to play for your delight,
Let love's table opened be.
Fear not, you are well matched
     with me.
Stake your maidenhead: you shall
     choose
Whether you will win or lose;
Or if you lose, I do believe
You will not for your loss once
     grieve. ❞**   *First published in 1640*

If all else fails, confuse them into surrender;

Boy: Is it true that most girls say 'yes' when they mean no, and say 'no' when they mean yes?

Girl: Yes/No

Boy: I thought so. Now, can I buy you a drink?

Girl: Yes/No

Boy: Good, what would you like?

Go up to her looking pretty upset, and say:

They say first impressions always last. I certainly hope that is not true for your sake, because my first impressions of you is one of hate, envy and resentment for having the power to make my heart ache like this. I guess some call it falling in love. Well what do you have to say for yourself?

Go up to the girl you wish to meet while the fast music is on and say;

Isn't it funny how most guys become very sociable when the slow dance starts. That's why I have come to you now to prove that my intentions are honourable, and that it is your heart and mind I wish to touch, and not your body.

This one needs courage and a straight face;

Yeh... you seem like the kind of earthling I could trust. You see I am from another planet. I have been sent down here on a mission to try and discover more about you and your planet. I have already found out what this thing, love is. It is like a comet landing on your head; it knocks you out senseless for a while. And marriage is like getting life imprisonment without actually commiting a crime, unless of course that comet lands on your head. What still puzzles me though is this thing called sex, which you all seem to be so preoccupied about. You see where I come from, sex is when you put your ten fingers on someone else's ten fingers and close your eyes for a while. Look... I'll show you. You see we have just had sex. Well... how was it for you? Now that I have shown you how we do it on our planet, how about you showing me how you do it on planet earth?

*If you are with some friends, and you see someone
you would like to meet, try this one;*

My friends over there have bet me £100
that I haven't got what it takes to chat
you up. So I was wondering if you could
help me win the bet, and make bigger
fools out of them than they tried to make
out of me. All you have to do is to pretend as though you are interested and
keep talking to me for a few minutes.

Meanwhile to show my appreciation, I
would be honoured if you would let me
buy you a drink.

Go up to the person you wish to meet and say:

I found this place very dull, empty and
hopelessly boring, until my eyes through
the clouds of smoke caught sight of your
beauty... and now that I am this close to
you, I can see why they say smoke can
damage more than just your heart and
lungs. It also distorts your vision, I can't
see a bloody thing.

*Have the following poem sent to the one you wish
to pass your telephone number to.*

Were I as base as the lowly plain,
And you my love, as high as heaven above
Yet should the thoughts of me your
   humble swain
Ascend to heaven, in honour of my love.

Were I as high as heaven above the plain
And you, my love as humble and as low
As are the deepest bottoms of the main
Where-so-ever you were, with you my
   love should go

Were you the earth dear love, and I the
   skies
My love should shine on you like to the
   sun.
And look upon you with ten thousand
   eyes
Till heaven went blind, and till world
   were done

Where-so-ever I am, below, or else above
   you
Where-so-ever you are, my heart shall
   truly love you.

Adapted from a poem by Joshua Sylvester 1611

Write the following message on a serviette and have it sent to her table;

Hello, my name is heart. I am in the body of that guy sitting over to your right. I am making the hand write this note against the wishes of the brain; because he does not think that this is the right thing to do. But I believe that an intelligent looking person like you can see that this is a genuine attempt to make a friend. So lets prove the brain wrong and be friends.

Go up to the guy you wish to meet and say;

Most guys are like lavatories;
They are vacant, engaged or full of crap.
Which one are you?

Try this one if you enjoy watching a guy lose his
cool and panic. Go to him and say;

If you want to have your wicked way with
me, all you have to do is ask.

Holding a bunch of flowers, go up to the girl you wish to meet and say;

If I were to give you these flowers and say, 'Men just can't help acting on impulse', you would probably take them, hit me on the head with them, and say 'women can't help acting on impulse either', Wouldn't you? That's why I am not giving them to you until you agree to have a drink with me, and if after that drink, your impulse is still the same, then I won't stand in your way.

If all else fails, try saying it in a poem:

Since all things love, why should not we,
The best of creature, be as free?
the pearl-eyed fish in every water
Pursues his love, being taught by nature.
The seely worm, the lamb, and harmless
    dove,
Which knoweth nothing, yet know how to
    love.

All senseless things love's passions feel,
The stone attracts the unyielding steel.
The ivy twines on every tree
And loves it more than you love me,
And in the cold of winter fresh is seen,
For heat of love is it that keeps it green.

Then learn by seeing what they do,
If they want eyes, hands, tongues, yet woo,
Can you that have of each the best,
Apt for that use, yet use them least?
It is sin to think the world did never yet
    show
So unkind a breast graced with so mild
    a brow.

(Continued)

Then let us love whilst we're in youth,
You fraught with beauty, I with truth,.
We'll make the world, being in our prime,
Wrinkled with envy more than time,
and when too old to live the fate draws
  nigh,
Our love shall make us too young to die.

Adapted from a poem by: Walter Porter 1632

party/club etc...   **41**

Taking a map of the world out of your pocket and showing it to her, you say:

  Stick with me girl, and I'll show you
  the world.

If you are sitting with some friends, and you see someone you would like to meet, go over to her and say;

You wouldn't believe the conversation they are having over there. I just had to get away. I said I have seen someone I know. So please could you pretend you know me. To show my appreciation, I would be honoured if you let me buy you a drink.

Go up to the girl you think may be interested in you, and say;

Look I have been watching you for the past ten minutes, and I think It's only fair to warn you that I am in fact a body language-therapist and have received every message your body has sent out. Now, you either tell your body to stop it, or else I will have no alternative but to take her up on them.

Go up to the girl you wish to meet, preferably someone who has just been dancing, and say;

I have been watching you dance, and since neither of us knows how to dance, I thought perhaps we could just have a drink and a chat.

Go up to the girl you wish to meet and say;

Someone once said that love is like measles; we all have to go through it. And since I am in love with the most beautiful creature on earth, I thought may be if I stick around her long enough there is a chance that she may catch it too. So have you seen a beautiful girl covered with spots? No... oh well you'll do.

If all else fails to get a little smile out of a beautiful face, then try sending her this poem;

> 66 I am very shy you see
> So help me if you can
> Throw a little smile at me
> And make me a happy man. 99

If you don't enjoy being turned down, then try this one;

> 66 When a lady says no
> She means may be
> When a lady says may be
> She means yes
> When a lady says yes
> She is no lady.
> So can I buy you a drink? 99

If all else fails, try raising her curosity, just to keep her interested long enough to impress her.

I have been doing a little research, trying to find out as much as I can about you. But everyone I have spoken to has said the same thing. I have now come over to find out what they have said is true. I can't tell you what it is. You will have to let me find out over a drink. If it is true, then I will tell you.

If her beauty has left you somewhat numb, try sending her this poem:

> **"** I have seen the sun rise and fall
> I have seen the trees grow so tall
> I have seen the sea caress the shores
> Even the wind blow through moores
> But beauty as you possess
> I haven't seen, I must confess
> So why not give me a closer look
> At the bait you threw which got
> me hooked
> If the answer is yes nod your head
> I'll come running so we can wed. **"**

*Holding a bottle of sun tan lotion, go up to the
girl you wish to meet and say;*

I know this is highly irregular, but I
wouldn't bother you if it wasn't a mat-
ter of life and death. You see if I don't
get medication on my back in the form
of sun tan oil, my skin will burn, caus-
ing my heart to beat faster, followed by
a stroke and a coma, and then who
knows...death. So please would you save
my life.

Look deep into her eyes and say;

To be in the presence of someone with beauty such as yours, is like a dream from which no man on earth would wish to be awakened. So how about letting me dream away for a while over a drink?

Send the following poem to that special someone;

❝ The things about you I adore
Are so many. No may be more.
I like your eyes, I like your nose
I like the way your lips disclose
I like your teeth, I like your hair
Even your tache I must declare
I like your legs, I like your arms
The way they come in pairs adds
to your charm
I like your face, I like your mind
Beauty as you possess is hard to find
I like to see you one more time
and more
To tell you more things about you
I adore
So what chat up line can I use?
Which would sparkle and light
your fuse
Oh I give up, I haven't got a clue
I haven't got one that is worthy of
you
If you can think of any please let
me know
I'll be waiting here so have a go. ❞

Go up to the person you wish to meet and say;

I could bore you to death with a carefully worked out chat up line which might
impress you or might bore you to surrender. Or I could come clean and say
that you are the most beautiful thing I
have seen for a long time, and would be
honoured if you let me buy you a drink.
Which will it be?

Go over to the girl you wish to meet and say,

I have been looking around all evening
for someone who knows both of us, so
that they could introduce us; but I
haven't found anyone. So I have decided
to do it myself. My name is..., my hob-
bies are ski-ing, deep sea diving? hand
gliding? and lying through my teeth.
But that's enough about me, tell me
about you.''

*Present a bunch of flowers to the girl you have been
wanting to meet for a while, and say;*

> You can forget all that 'men just can't
> help acting on impulse' business. This is
> not impulse. I have seen you many times,
> but could never build up enough courage
> to come and talk to you incase you shat-
> tered all my dreams. But now that I have
> said my piece, I can handle the rejection,
> because at lease now you know of this
> great love I have for you.''

*Have the following poem sent to the one you wish
to kiss;*

“ The fountains mingle with the river
   And the rivers with the ocean,
   The winds of heaven mix forever
   With a sweet emotion;
   Nothing in the world is single,
   All things by a law divine
   In one another's being mingle-
   Why not I with thine?

   See the mountains kiss high
   heaven
   And the waves clasp one another;
   No sister flower would be forgiven
   If it disdained its brother
   And the sunlight clasps the earth,
   And the moonbeams kiss the sea,
   What are all these kissings worth,
   If thou kiss not me?

   So to arrange a kiss for love
   Smile is all you have to do;
   And I will fly like a dove
   To present my lips to you

Adapted from a poem by Percy Bysshe Shelley 1814

If you find a beautiful girl sitting on her own, try this one; but make sure that her solitude is of her own choosing and that you are not putting salt on a wound.

My friends and I were thinking that it is not right for a girl like you to be sitting on her own, so we drew straws to see who should ask you to dance. I lost, so here I am.

*She is alone, but very happy relaxing in the sun.
You go over and offer to help. What a gallant
display.*

I realise that there is nothing more an-
noying when you are trying to have a lie
in the sun when a complete idiot comes
over and starts talking to you. So I
thought I'd come over and sit here just
in case an idiot does come along, I could
scare them away.

Meanwhile you can look upon me as your
personal bodyguard, so please feel free
to ask me anything you wish to know
about the security service I provide.

Go up to the one you wish to meet, raise your hand, and like a red Indian say:

How

She will probably reply in the same gesture:

How

Then continue by saying:

Now that we have discovered how, lets work out where and when.

Go up to the guy you like to meet and say;

I don't usually make a habit of approaching guys. But you strike me as being very shy; And since someone once said that the two lonliest people are shy men and beautiful women, I thought I'd come over and put both of us out of our miseries.

*Take a bunch of flowers over to the girl you wish
to impress, and say;*

I hope you don't mind, but I have
brought these flowers over so that they
could see what real beauty looks like.

Can I stick around while you teach them
a thing or two?

Go up to the girl you wish to meet, and say:

I may not be tall dark and handsome and
I may not have a great taste in clothes,
but at least I have nerve to try anything,
even the impossible, which is exactly what
this plea for friendship is turning out to
be.

O.K. let me start again...

I may not be...

Oh the hell with it, can I buy you a
drink?

telephone exchange   *63*

If you prefer to break the ice over the telephone, try this:

❝ Were you a fish, I would swim
The seven seas for you
Were you a bird, I would fly
To the skies for you
Were you to phone, my number now
Who knows what I wouldn't do for you?

park/street   *64*

If the girl you wish to meet looks the shy type, go up to her and say:

You have a choice: you can either let me buy you a drink peacefully, or I'll embarrass you by singing John Travolta's 'You Are the One That I Want', very loudly until you give in. So what will it be?

Find out what current or forthcoming concert/theatre etc. she would like to go to, buy some tickets, go up to her and say;

I have two tickets for the concert/theatre and I can't think of anyone I would rather go with than you, so I was wondering if you have no other plans, may be you'd like to go with me and make the evening that little bit extra special.

Try keeping a straight face when you use this one:

I was wondering if you could help me..
As you can probably see, I have been put
under a spell, and made to look like this
disgusting creature that you can see
before you. I am destined to look like this
for the rest of my life, unless of course,
the spell can be broken, and I will turn
back to the tall dark and handsome hunk
that I used to be.
Now, I am told that the only way to have
this spell broken, is to be kissed by a
beautiful girl... so will you help me?

*If the first kiss doesn't break the spell, ask her to
try and try again.*

If you see a shop assistant you wish to meet or take out, go up to her and try this line. It would help if whatever she is selling is the sort of thing one buys ladies for presents.

I was wondering if you could help me. I would like to buy a present for some one I haven't yet met, to break the ice and kind of ask her out for a drink. Would you help me choose a present which would impress her so much that she couldn't refuse my invitation?

Then once she has chosen the present, ask her to wrap it up, pay for it and finally give it to her, asking her out at the same time.

bar/club 68

Go up to the girl you wish to have a drink with, and say:

> Today women give up too easily, I think they should play harder to get. Now, can I buy you a drink?
> You see that's exactly what I mean... what did you say 'no'. Come on I didn't mean play that hard.

bar/club 69

Go up to the girl/boy you have fallen for, and say;

> The maddening thing about love is that one can never synchronise one's watches. Like right now for instance: I have fallen madly in love with you, and yet you haven't even begun to like me. So would you like a little time to catch up?

club/sport centre   70

If you need a nod of approval or a wink before you make your move, try this;

> You are cute lovely and fair
> I want to ask you out, but I don't dare
> You see, I cannot take a rejection
> I hate it as much as an injection
> So please please send me a sign
> To let me know you will be mine.

club/sports centre   71

Choose your victim carefully for this one;

> At your age I bet your diary is
> crammed full of names and telephone
> numbers;
> Doctors, Psychiartrists, Clinics, Health
> Farms, Slimming Clubs
> So here's mine to add to your list as
> your very own toy boy.

Go over to a beautiful princess sitting all alone, and say;

O.K. here I am... Oh no please don't tell me there's been some kind of mistake again. You see, your fairy Godmother sent me. She said that there is a beautiful girl down there, sitting all alone, wishing she had someone to talk to, someone who could bring a little smile to that pretty face of hers. But judging by your reaction it seems she made a mistake, and sent me too soon, and I guess I better be on my way... unless of course I could just stick around until you finally decide to make that wish.
How about it?

If after a while, she still hasn't noticed you, try this one;

Of all the greatest love stories, ours must be the saddest. The story of a guy passionately in love, blinded by the girl's beauty, overcome by her presence. And the girl, though very beautiful, intelligent and highly sensitive just doesn't know he exists.

I wouldn't like to be in your shoes, having to choose an ending to this story; A sad ending where she refuses to have a drink with him, and he becomes so devastated that he spends the rest of his life in the gutter, drunk.

Or a happy ending where she agrees to have a drink with him, and he in return promises to give her flowers, chocolates and presents every day.

If you find yourself waiting for the bus with a beautiful girl, try this one:

Do you realise that everything we do, every situation we come across has all been written down and is our fate. The fact that we should be waiting for the bus at the same time is all fate. The fact that you are ignoring my genuine offer of friendship, maybe that someone just wanted you to go through life without the most sensitive, loving and kind companion.

Do you want to change your fate?

You adore her, but she hasn't noticed you. Go up to her and recite this poem.

  ❝ I have seen you many times
      But never had the guts
      To tell you how I feel
      For its lots and lots and lots

      So can I buy you a drink
      to show you how I feel?
      If you show me the way you blink
      I'll even buy the meal. **❞**

Make sure she/he has a sense of humour for this one;

Most worthwhile and lasting friendships always start with a few simple words. And as soon as I laid eyes on you, I knew that you are the sort of person I would love to have as a friend. So I have come over to utter those simple words: **Can I borrow a fiva?**

*As already mentioned, of all the paths that lead
to a woman's love, pity is the straightest. If that's
true then try this one;*

" Come, pretty wanton, tell me why
You cannot love as well as I.
Sit you down, sit you down, and
you shall see
Why thus unkind you are to me.

My dearest sweet, be not so coy,
For you alone are all my joy.
Sit you down, sit you down, and
you shall see
That it is high time to pity me.

O gentle love, be not yet gone.
Leave me not her distressed alone.
Sit you down, sit you down, and
you shall see
That I delight in none but thee.

Let me not cry to thee in pain.
Look but upon me once again.
If a look, if a look, you will not
lend,
Let but your gentle ears attend.

continued

If you do stop those gentle ears
Look but upon these cruel tears,
Which do force me still to cry
Pity me, sweet, or else I die. **"**

Adapted from a poem by William Herbert 1660

party 78

Go up to her and say;

Look, you are a nice girl
I am a nice guy
Would you like to take a shower?

Just hope that the person you try this one on is not too touchy about her age;

Hi, my name is…, I have been sent from the Toy Boy Agency. It seems from the specification you gave, the computer finally picked me for you. I am young, fertile, with good physique and extremely handsome; and I love older, more mature women like yourself. So how would you like to accept the agency's free seven day home trial?

Go up to the guy you wish to meet, and say;

You seem to have got yourself a reputation here. They say you are different from all the other guys; You don't act like a dirty old man. You are a dirty old man. So I have come over to give you a chance to prove them all wrong.

Go up to the one you wish to dance with, and ask her in a poem;

> **66 Can I have this dance with you**
> **Cause its you I adore**
> **Can I feel my arms around you**
> **Like sea around the shore**
> **I wrote this poem to ask you to dance**
> **I know its bad, but give me a chance.**

Although this one has a safety net built in to prevent embarrassment you may still get a thick ear.

I have come over to tell you that you are the most beautiful thing I have seen for a long time, and I would be honoured if you let me buy you a drink... or at least walk me to the bar, cause I've left my contact lenses at home; and I can't see a bloody thing without them.

If the girl of your dreams appears somewhat glum, try this:

No wonder its so dark here... you are not smiling. Look I am fed up with knocking into things, and I know that all the lights in the world couldn't light up a room the way your smile can. So how about a little smile, just to give me enough light to see my way to the bar and buy you a drink.

If all else fails try sympathy;

They say of all the paths that lead to a
girl's love — pity is the straightest. Well,
did you know that I was born an orphan,
I never had the love, the love of a mother
holding her child. The love of a father,
that tender love which everyone takes for
granted. I have always been alone; with
no relatives or friends of my own. But
now I have finally found, found the
person who could replace all this missing
love... You. You are my last chance, my
only hope for survival. Oh but what is
the use. I can see you are going to reject
me too, like the rest of the human race.
I guess I just have to die in search of love.
What do you think?

Go up to the one you wish to meet and say;

> **Excuse me, I know this is a little strange,
> but I am celebrating a happy event, and
> would be honoured if you would join me
> in my celebration, and have a drink with
> me.**

*Do not disclose the happy event, until you have
fixed a date, then reveal that the happy event was
the fact that you managed to fool someone with
the celebrating gag.*

Go up to the guy you wish to scare, and say;

Us women have put up with you men for
years, coming up to us with lousy chat
up lines, and we have to pretend that we
are impressed. So I have decided to come
over and show you how it should really
be done.
'Will you marry me?'

Go up to the guy you wish to meet and say;

I don't think it is fair that men have
always been the ones accepted in society
to make the first move, That's why I have
come over to tell you that you can buy
me a drink.

Go over to her and recite the following poem;

> ❝ I love you, I love you
> that's all I can say
> It is my vision in the night
> And my dreaming in the day
> Can I buy you a drink
> O... please say I may
> I promise not to bore you
> If you promise to pay. ❞

Try this one if you are over seven feet tall, or else enjoy getting a clip around the ear;

> ❝ They say sex is very much like
> gardening:
> Sometimes its big
> Sometimes its small
> Sometimes you get nothing at all.
> But you play your cards right and
> you have nothing to worry about.
> Cause I have green fingers. ❞

Make sure she understands the importance of your request;

do you know what Eve said to Adam when he started chatting her up. She said: 'I wouldn't go out with you if you were the last person on earth.' No actually, she didn't say that, but imagine what would have happened if she had said that. You and I would not be here for a start.

So if I asked you to have a drink with me, would that be too much to ask for the sake of the future generations?

If you find yourself left alone in the company of someone with whom you have shared all the right signs, then try this one;

Don't be embarrassed. It is quite natural. They say that at the beginning of love, and at its end, the lovers are embarrassed to be left alone.
If you like we can skip the beginning, and pretend we have known each other for a while. So how is your Mum doing now?

Send the following message to the girl who has not yet noticed you;

❝ a smile it is a funny thing
it wrinkles up your face
And when its gone, you never find
its secret hiding place

But far more wonderful it is
To see what a smile can bring
You smile at one – he smiles at you
and so begins that special thing. ❞

If you feel that your looks are not a good selling point, try this;

They say a man falls in love through his eyes, and a woman through her ears. So here it goes: your beauty is heaven sent. Let me look at you, let me memorise that beauty, so I can dream. Dream of your lips touching my face like fire on my cheeks. Dream of your perfume like fire in my mind. Dream of you holding me with your arms like chains. Chains of fire about my body. Dream of your body aching for mine. Aching to surrender itself. Are you in love yet? O.K. listen to this. I am actually a millionaire I have a yacht, a private jet and villas around the world. I would buy you diamonds everyday. How am I doing?

Go up to the girl who has just been dancing, and say:

Excuse me. The management have asked me to come over and talk to you about your conduct in this establishment. They are no longer willing to let you in if you insist on not learning to dance properly. So they have asked me to come over, as the resident dance teacher to discuss with you the free dance lessons they are offering to certain special customers. So if you follow me to the bar, we can talk about the details over a drink.

*While walking your dog, you come across an at-
tractive girl walking her dog. As soon as the dogs
start getting to know one another, your line could
go something like this;*

Last time I saw my dog look so happy
was after Lassie was on the telly, and
there was a bark outside the front door,
he thought Lassie had come to see him.
You know I can actually tell what my dog
is thinking just by looking at him. At the
moment he is saying 'I just hope our
owners stick around long enough for us
to get to know each other a bit better.'
So what do you say to sacrificing a few
minutes of our time for the sake of a
promising love affair amongst two poor
dumb animals. I am sure our dogs would
enjoy it too.

Two dozen white roses and this poem may just be enough to make that special someone notice you;

I love snow and all the forms
Of the radiant frost;
I love waves, and winds, and storms,
Everything almost.

I love tranquil solitude,
And such society
As is quiet, wise, and good;
Between thee and me

I love love – though it has wings,
And like light it can flee,
But above all other things,
My love, I love thee

Take this as my attempt to break
the ice
The rest is up to thee
What I have to say are not lies,
But what I give to you for free.

You are love and life, oh come
Make for ever my heart thy home.

Adapted from a poem by Percy Bysshe Shelley 1814

Some girls love being teased about their age. If you ever come across one in her early twenties, try this one on her:

You are my kind of girl.
You are flirty, dirty and over thirty.
Can I buy you a drink, cause I am
sporty, Naughty and over forty.

You need a photograph of yourself handy for this one;

> I am sorry to bother you, but I work in a dating agency; and we have this client who is suave, sophisticated, rich and very good looking. He has given a description of the girl he like to meet. At first glance, you fit that description. I was therefore wondering whether I could show you his picture, so that you can see if you would like to meet him. Before I show you his picture, I must say that he is a compulsive lier, and would go to any lengths to have a drink with the girl of his dreams.

Then show her the picture of yourself.

If you enjoy proposing, try this one;

Look, I realise that we are complete
strangers; but as soon as I saw you I felt
the urge to come over and ask you to
marry me. I know you will enjoy being
married to me. You see, I come from a
long line of married people. My Mum
and Dad were married, their Mum and
Dad were married too. Even my Great
Grandparents were married. All my
Aunts and Uncles are married. So I will
just be continuing the family tradition.

Hold this book up to reveal the cover. Then while turning the pages as if you were looking for an appropriate   line   to   use,   say;

> **Ah... no not that one... oh yeh...**
> **... oh no... ah... hang on... ah...**

Then throwing the book away, say;

> **Oh the hell with it. My name is... and**
> **I would be honoured if you would let me**
> **buy you a drink.**

telephone numbers

Name: ....

Telephone Number: ....

Marks out of ten: ....

Name: ....

Telephone Number: ....

Marks out of ten: ....

Name: ....

Telephone Number: ....

Marks out of ten: ....

Name: ....

Telephone Number: ....

Marks out of ten: ....

Name: ....

Telephone Number: ....

Marks out of ten: ....

Name: ....

Telephone Number: ....

Marks out of ten: ....

Name: ....

Telephone Number: ....

Marks out of ten: ....

Name: ....

Telephone Number: ....

Marks out of ten: ....

Name: ....

Telephone Number: ....

Marks out of ten: ....

Name: ....

Telephone Number: ....

Marks out of ten: ....

Name: ....

Telephone Number: ....

Marks out of ten: ....

Name: ....

Telephone Number: ....

Marks out of ten: ....

Name: . . . .

Telephone Number: . . . .

Marks out of ten: . . . .

Name: . . . .

Telephone Number: . . . .

Marks out of ten: . . . .

Name: . . . .

Telephone Number: . . . .

Marks out of ten: . . . .

Name: . . . .

Telephone Number: . . . .

Marks out of ten: . . . .

Name: ....

Telephone Number: ....

Marks out of ten: ....

Name: ....

Telephone Number: ....

Marks out of ten: ....

Name: ....

Telephone Number: ....

Marks out of ten: ....

Name: ....

Telephone Number: ....

Marks out of ten: ....

Name: . . . .

Telephone Number: . . . .

Marks out of ten: . . . .

Name: . . . .

Telephone Number: . . . .

Marks out of ten: . . . .

Name: . . . .

Telephone Number: . . . .

Marks out of ten: . . . .

Name: . . . .

Telephone Number: . . . .

Marks out of ten: . . . .

100 CHAT UP LINES

A pocket size reference book packed with one hundred original, romantic, humourous, witty, poetic, sarcastic, and even some down right pretentious chat up lines for every occasion. Some illustrated with sketches for quick reference. (128 pages).

Fill in the coupon below and send it with your payment to:
IDEAS UNLIMITED, P.O. BOX 125 PORTSMOUTH PO1 4PP.

Please send me .... copy/copies of '100 Chat Up Lines' at £2 each. I have enclosed a cheque/PO for £ .... made payable to Ideas Unlimited.

Name: (BLOCK CAPITALS PLEASE)

. . . .

Address: (BLOCK CAPITALS PLEASE)

. . . .

---

100 CHAT UP LINES

A pocket size reference book packed with one hundred original, romantic, humourous, witty, poetic, sarcastic, and even some down right pretentious chat up lines for every occasion. Some illustrated with sketches for quick reference. (128 pages).

Fill in the coupon below and send it with your payment to:

IDEAS UNLIMITED, P.O. BOX 125 PORTSMOUTH PO1 4PP.

---

100 CHAT UP LINES

A pocket size reference book packed with one hundred original, romantic, humourous, witty, poetic, sarcastic, and even some down right pretentious chat up lines for every occasion. Some illustrated with sketches for quick reference. (128 pages).

Fill in the coupon below and send it with your payment to:
IDEAS UNLIMITED, P.O. BOX 125
PORTSMOUTH PO1 4PP.

Please send me .... copy/copies of '100 Chat Up Lines' at £2 each. I have enclosed a cheque/PO for £ .... made payable to Ideas Unlimited.

Name: (BLOCK CAPITALS PLEASE)

. . . .

Address: (BLOCK CAPITALS PLEASE)

. . . .
